020

D0297764

4892

991762001 X

On the Home Front

On the Home Front

Growing Up in Wartime England

by Ann Stalcup

Linnet Books
1998

Library of Congress Cataloging-in-Publication Data

Stalcup, Ann, 1935–
On the home front : growing up in wartime England
/ by Ann Stalcup.
p. cm.
Includes bibliographical references (p.).
Summary: An account of a young child living in Lydney, England,
during World War II including memories of air raids,
gas masks, rationing, and war news as well as
routines of family, friends, and school.
ISBN 0-208-02482-4 (alk. paper)
1. Stalcup, Ann, 1935–   —Juvenile literature.
2. World War, 1939–1945—Personal narratives,
British—Juvenile literature.
3. Children—England—Lydney—Biography
—Juvenile literature.   4. Lydney (England)—History
—Juvenile literature.   [1. Stalcup, Ann, 1935–   .
2. World War, 1939–1945—Personal narratives, British.
3. England—History.]   I. Title.
D811.5.S717   1998
940.54′8141—dc21   97-32673
CIP
AC

The paper in this publication meets the minimum requirements
of American National Standard for Information Sciences—
Permanence of Paper for Printed Library Materials,
ANSI Z39.48—1984. ∞

Designed by Abigail Johnston

Printed in the United States of America

To my parents, Elsie and Joe Hotchkiss,
who throughout my life were loving and supportive.
How I wish they had lived long enough
to see this book published.
And to my husband, Ed,
whose help and encouragement have been invaluable.

Contents

Contents

Acknowledgments

With special thanks to Trish Charles, my editor, for pulling information from my memory that had long lain dormant, and for the dimension added by her own interest in, and knowledge of, both England and the Second World War.

My appreciation goes as well to these friends for sharing their wartime memories with me: Kath Windsor, whose family anecdotes added greatly to my book; Tom Wilcox, for sharing with me his rescue by the Little Ships from the beaches of Dunkirk; Ann Smithcors, who reminded me of black armbands and silent church bells; Ernie Nelmes, for telling me of his experiences as a prisoner of war in Germany; Jean and Maud Barnes, for providing price comparisons from 1945; Hilda Fogelson, for sharing her experience of being a nine-year-old Jewish child in Berlin in 1939, and her escape to England on one of the *Kindertransports*; and to my parents, Elsie and Joe Hotchkiss, who, long ago, when my book began as a college paper, reminded me of many half-remembered incidents from my wartime childhood.

Europe, 1939, with the author's home town of Lydney near the Severn River
marked by a dark arrow.

Introduction

In September 1938, a whole year before the Second World War would start, things began to change in England for everyone. My father joined the Air Raid Patrol, which people usually referred to as "the A.R.P." He attended meetings in the evenings so that he could learn what to do if Germany declared war on Britain and our town were bombed. In London, 120 miles away, two million people were told to be ready to leave the city if war started.

That same month, the British government issued a gas mask to each man, woman, and child. The masks looked like pigs' snouts and smelled foul. As a three-year-old, I was terrified when I tried mine on, so Mum hid them away and tried to convince me that we'd never have to wear them. Everyone worried that German planes would drop poisonous bombs over Britain. If they did, wearing the masks would protect people from the horrible gas.

London is the capital of Great Britain and is its largest

and most important city. Close to eight million people lived there in 1938, including King George, the queen, and their two young daughters, Princess Elizabeth and Princess Margaret Rose. Elizabeth is now Britain's queen.

Birmingham is another large city. It is north of London in the middle of England. Other cities surround it, and because of the many factories, the area is know as the "Industrial Midlands." The government was certain that when the Nazis started to drop bombs on England, London and Birmingham would be their primary targets. Many of the factories in Birmingham were now making bombs and airplanes instead of china or whatever they used to produce. It would help Hitler win the war if he could successfully destroy those factories. And if a lot of people were killed in London and Birmingham, the Nazi government could hope that the British people might lose their courage and surrender.

My four grandparents lived in Birmingham, and so did all of my aunts, uncles, and cousins. In the spring of 1939, six months before the war started, one of my grandmothers wrote to Mum and Dad about what people in Birmingham were doing to prepare for war. She said that trenches were being dug in the parks so people could hide in them if bombs were dropped. Many trenches had metal covers to make them safer. Some families preferred to dig holes in their back gardens. Then large concrete boxes called "Anderson Shelters" were lowered into the holes. They were covered with corrugated iron roofs and even had seats in them.

Introduction

We saw my grandparents' Anderson Shelter when we visited Birmingham in July 1939. It looked very small, damp, and cold, and I hoped I'd never have to spend time in it. The war still hadn't started, but in the air beyond their garden, all across a rugby football field, hovered some huge, sinister, silvery-gray things called "barrage balloons." They were firmly attached to the ground by steel cables, which sang whenever the wind blew. Their purpose was to prevent enemy planes from diving low to drop bombs on the cities. When we rode on buses in and out of the city center, we saw more of them. They filled the sky in every direction.

In London, in the years just before the outbreak of war, twenty thousand families owned a brand-new invention called a television set. At that time, television was still in the experimental stages in both Britain and the United States. In London, on September 1, 1939, in the middle of a Mickey Mouse cartoon, a printed message came onto everyone's screen. It said that all children and mothers with babies should evacuate London immediately. After the announcement, the world's first television station closed down and didn't reopen until several years after the war. That same day the wireless (radio) told the women and children of Birmingham that they needed to evacuate, too. Many people had already left both cities, but now evacuation became much more urgent. Britain was on the brink of war.

News broadcasts on the wireless were almost continuous, and families listened to the news for hours at a time.

Everyone was anxious to know exactly what was happening and whether the danger was getting closer. In those days right before war was declared, we were all nervous. If we wanted to see, instead of hear, what was happening, we had to go to the cinema (movies). Black and white newsreels called "Movietone News," containing actual scenes from the war, were shown before each feature film.

Between June 1939 and the first week of the war in September 1939, three and a half million people moved to towns and villages in the English countryside. As a four-year-old, it was hard for me to imagine what this meant. It sounded like such an enormous number. These children and a few mothers with babies were transported all over England, Scotland, and Wales by buses and trains. Two out of every three children left London, but only a quarter of the children left Birmingham. Birmingham was a greater distance from Germany, so the people who lived there believed that their city would be safer than London. Because I lived in the country already, I didn't have to be evacuated, but it was quite possible that we would soon be sharing our home with evacuees.

1939

We Are at War

On Sunday, September 3, 1939, at 11:00 A.M., Britain declared war on Nazi Germany. At 11:27 A.M. the first air raid siren wailed across London. We heard its mournful, chilling sound over the wireless, which we listened to all that day. The announcer said that eight million Londoners trooped down the steps of their garden air raid shelters. Others ran to the safety of the deep underground railway stations.

King George spoke to the nation on the wireless. His voice was trembling. At the end of the speech, he announced, "We are at war." Hearing these words gave me a funny feeling in my stomach. I was scared! I knew that King George and his two little princesses lived in London. I wondered if the princesses had heard about the war and if they were scared, too.

Mum and Dad tried to explain to me why we were at war. They said that Germany, under its Nazi leader, Adolf

Hitler, had invaded and taken over the country of Czechoslovakia in Europe. Then, on September 1, German troops
moved into Poland. Mr. Chamberlain, our country's prime
minister, had promised to help Poland if it were invaded.
He gave Hitler an ultimatum: Germany had until 11:00
A.M. on September 3, 1939, to pull out of Poland. Hitler
refused, so Britain had declared war.

After the First World War a political party called the
"National Socialist Workers' Party" began to gain popularity
in Germany. Its members were known as "Nazis," and their
symbol was the swastika. In 1933, Hitler rose to power as
the leader of the party, and he and his supporters seized
control of the government. Important people were required
to become Nazis, whether they supported Hitler's views or
not. His dream was to create what he called a superior, all-
white "master race" by eliminating all those he considered
unsuitable.

Hitler focused his anger on the Jews. Many were ar-
rested and imprisoned before the war started. Their busi-
nesses were taken away from them, their homes and stores
damaged, and their synagogues burned. Much of this occurred on the infamous *Kristallnacht* on November 9, 1938,
so named because of the amount of glass (*kristall*) that was
broken on that night (*nacht*). Since Hitler's ideal Germans
were fair-skinned and blonde-haired, the Nazis were suspi-
cious of anyone with dark hair or skin, often making the
assumption that they were Jewish.

Many Germans did not support the Nazis, but defying the government was a dangerous business. People, whether they were Jewish or not, became afraid to trust neighbors or even best friends. Those who criticized the government risked being reported as traitors. Everyone, Nazi supporter or not, had to raise his arm in a stiff-armed salute and say, "Heil Hitler!" when someone saluted him. Failure to do so could lead to arrest.

For weeks the grownups at home and in the shops had been whispering together. I'd heard the word "war" more and more often, but if I tried to ask questions, they changed the subject. Mum and Dad only said that they did not want to worry me. They told me I was too young to understand what was happening. They always seemed so serious now. War obviously meant that things would be a lot different.

When the war began, I was four and living with my mum and dad in the small country town of Lydney in the west of England. Our house was surrounded by fields filled with sheep and cows, and there were no cities nearby. We didn't have iron and concrete bomb shelters or trenches in which to hide, but every house had wide strips of brown tape pasted onto its windows in crisscross patterns. Mum said that if a bomb dropped nearby, the tape would keep the windows from shattering and hurting someone.

Once war was declared, we had to black out our house at night like everyone else in Britain. Every window had to be covered with thick black curtains. During the whole month of August, Mum had been busy making them. Outside, the summer days were bright and sunny. It seemed as if nothing had changed. But whenever I went indoors, the sewing machine was still whirring.

And there was black material everywhere! Sometimes Mum asked me to help her measure out the material. I wished I were older and knew how to use a sewing machine so that I could make some of the curtains for her. Then it wouldn't have taken Mum so many days to finish them. I missed playing with her and talking to her. There never seemed to be time for that now.

Each night, from sunset to sunrise, everyone's black curtains had to be tightly closed. Policemen and air raid wardens like my dad checked all the houses every night. If anyone had a chink of light showing, they had to pay a fine. Mum explained that if the Nazis started to bomb England, the British government wanted all of the cities and towns to be invisible from the air. There were no street lights, and drivers weren't allowed to turn on their car headlights. If you went out after dark, you couldn't even use a flashlight.

It was so dark outdoors during the evenings that people tried not to go out at all. During the first weeks of the war, we heard lots of sad stories about people being killed or injured badly in road accidents because cars and pedestrians couldn't see each other. Some people fell down steps or into canals and rivers; some stepped off railway platforms onto the railway lines. Almost every night my dad had to go out on his A.R.P. rounds. Unless it was a bright moonlit night, it was hard for him to find his way safely. We worried about him until he came home.

Like most families in England in those days, we didn't have a car, but for those who did, it was a difficult time. After a while there were special hoods for headlights and for flashlights that made it easier to get around after dark. Soon "cats' eyes" were invented. Two glass balls the size of marbles were set into each side of a flexible rubber casing. Placed on the center line of the busiest roads, they reflected the dim light from the hooded headlights. They made driving so much safer on Britain's winding roads, and from the air, they were invisible.

1939

Evacuees

Even though I was only four at the time, I remember the evacuation very clearly. On September 8, only five days after what was called the "outbreak of war," my family life changed completely: The first two of our evacuees arrived. Jackie and Judy were eleven. One had dark hair, and one was blonde. They would be going to classes in Lydney when the school year began in a few days. Along with Jackie and Judy came a crotchety, bad-tempered, feisty little teacher named Miss Thomas. All three of our evacuees came to Lydney from Yardley Grammar School (high school). Yardley was one of Birmingham's many suburbs.

Yardley sent 277 students and 32 teachers to Lydney. My dad was a chemistry teacher at Lydney Grammar School, and life really changed for him. The Lydney students went to school from 9:00 A.M. to 1:00 P.M.; the Yardley students and their teachers had school from 1:30 P.M. to 5:30 P.M. My dad had the afternoons off, but the

Lydney students and teachers had to go to school on Saturdays. The Yardley students did not. The Lydney teenagers were very unhappy about that, and so was my dad. I hated it, too. Instead of playing with me on Saturday mornings before going off for a round of golf with his friends, he had to go to work. On Sundays he always went to church and then was too busy doing schoolwork to spend time with me.

The Yardley students weren't the only evacuees who came to Lydney. Younger children came, too, and a few mothers with babies. Thousands of others were being scattered all over Great Britain. We heard that when the children in London and Birmingham poured onto the railway platforms in September, they were pushed and pulled into whatever train happened to be available. It was days before some parents knew where their children had been sent.

Mum told me that the children who traveled by train had terrible journeys. The trains were very crowded. Many had no toilets, and only a little food was available. When we met our Yardley students at the train station in Lydney, we saw a lot of dirty, weeping, frightened, and exhausted children. Many were as young as I was. All of them wore labels around their necks. If they were traveling with a school, their label had the name of the school in large letters; otherwise, it had the child's name and address. Our visit to the train station made me very glad that I didn't have to be evacuated.

Whole schools traveled together, just as the Yardley

school had, but we heard that brothers and sisters and friends got separated as they changed from train to train or bus to bus. Children were delivered to the wrong houses in the wrong towns. It took a long time to get them all sorted out.

Some of the homes that expected to have young children got mothers and babies instead. Evacuees sometimes had to stay in temporary shelters, like town halls, for days because too many people had been sent to the same place. There were no blankets or beds and hardly any food for them. It all sounded awful to me.

Lydney was no different from the other places where evacuees were sent. When trains arrived at the station, farmers were waiting to pick out the strongest looking boys. They wanted boys who could help them on their farms because most of the workers had already left to become soldiers. Ladies with big houses wanted teenagers to mind their children and help with the housework. Wealthy people picked the best-dressed children. No one wanted the ragged, dirty ones.

Some of the elderly men in our town who had always lived alone suddenly found themselves caring for four or five children. Mr. Archibald, an unmarried man who lived on our hill, didn't know what to do with the little children who were sent to stay with him. He said they were noisy and never stopped eating. He was very unhappy about it. After a while, several evacuated teachers moved in with Mr. Archibald, and his children went to live with someone else. He was much happier, especially since one of the teachers did all of the cooking.

We heard that many of the children who came from the poorer parts of Birmingham and London had never seen toothbrushes, bathtubs, indoor toilets, or bed sheets. In fact, some had always slept on the floor rather than in real beds. By contrast, some of the children from nice homes in the city now lived with farm workers who used the fields and bushes as their toilets. Their only running water was a tap outside. Many of these children had never been to the country before and didn't even know that milk came from cows and eggs came from chickens. It must have been very hard to adjust to the strangeness. Mum and Dad treated our evacuees the same as they treated me, although it was much harder to be nice to cranky Miss Thomas.

Soon two more evacuees came to live with us. They were my cousin Audrey, who was four years old like me, and a girl named Edna, who was a bit older. Audrey was from Birmingham, and Edna was from London. Except for the awful Miss Thomas, the war suddenly seemed rather wonderful to me. There had been no children living nearby, and I now had two friends of my own age to play with all day long. We would be starting school in January, but in the meantime, what fun we had playing with our dolls and having endless make-believe tea parties. And it seemed to be hot and sunny every day.

Once school began, Jackie and Judy had lots of homework to do, so we didn't see much of them. They spent most of their time in their room. When they appeared at the table for meals, they never talked much. We all worked very hard to make them feel welcome, but I'm sure they were terribly homesick for their families.

Miss Thomas was another matter. Whenever she appeared, always dressed in brown from head to toe, she was like a dark cloud. Nothing was ever right for her: Her bed was too soft; we children were too noisy. No matter how hard my mum tried, Miss Thomas complained about every meal. She never seemed to realize that there was less and less food available and that Mum was doing her best. Poor Jackie and Judy. They had to put up with her at school, too.

1940

The Phoney War

The Nazi leader, Adolf Hitler, had expected to invade Britain by Christmas of 1939, but for a long time no bombs fell, and no one from Britain was fighting anywhere. Still, things at home *were* different! For one thing, now there was only one wireless station instead of two, and war news was broadcast every hour. It was almost impossible for me, or anyone else, to think about anything but the war.

The government called this time the "Phoney War" because nothing much happened. The evacuated children missed their parents, so all over the country, they began to return home. Jackie and Judy went back to Birmingham after six months, and soon after that, Edna and my cousin Audrey left, too. They were both homesick, and their parents were lonely without them. It seemed very quiet after they left.

Later in the war, when the bombing of the cities was at its worst, evacuees were sent out of the cities again. Some returned to the families they had lived with before. For many families, the homesickness had been very bad when the children had left for the country earlier. Now they decided to stay together, no matter how dangerous it became.

The lucky families who had relatives in Canada, the United States, Australia, South Africa, or New Zealand sent their children by sea to spend the war there in safety. Other parents, desperate to get their children out of England, got special permits to send them to Canada, where accommodations were found for them when they arrived. But it was a dangerous journey. Some of the boats carrying evacuees were torpedoed, in spite of the huge convoy of small warships that traveled with them.

Unfortunately, grumpy Miss Thomas stayed for twelve long months. She hardly ever said anything pleasant to anyone, so it was an endless year. The highlight of my time with Miss Thomas was quite unexpected. My mum and I were taking Miss Thomas on a shortcut to town. The shortcut took us through a muddy farmyard. Trying to avoid a particularly wet, sticky patch, Miss Thomas stepped sideways onto a metal grate covering a water-filled drain. The grill collapsed, and Miss Thomas disappeared up to her waist. She was soaking wet, and badly shocked, and definitely not amused. But we were! Witnessing her fury and distress that day almost made our year of misery with her worth it.

In January 1940 I had started school along with Audrey and Edna. I was four and a half then. The walk to school was over a mile, and since it was uphill all the way home,

coming back seemed even further. No hot lunches were
served at school, so we came home at lunchtime, too. Lunch
was always the main meal of the day. When Audrey and
Edna went home at the end of March, I no longer had anyone to talk with, which made each journey seem endless.

We carried our gas masks to school every day in a box
with a shoulder strap. Each morning we practiced wearing
them for a few minutes before our lessons began. We all
looked so ridiculous that we usually ended up laughing and
giggling, or snorting like pigs, since the masks were so pig-
like. It was hard for the teacher to control the class after that.

The mask covered your entire face and had an oblong
window for your eyes. The snout itself had two black holes
in it. A strap went around the back of your head. When I
put mine on, the smell was so awful that I was always afraid
that I was going to be sick inside it.

By this time, special gas masks had been invented for
infants. My friend's mum had one for her new baby. The
baby was enclosed in a cradle-like covered box. One end of
the lid, where the baby's head would be, was a clear plastic
dome. Air was pumped into it with a bellows. It must have
been terrifying for the baby.

For a while after the gas masks were first issued, the
grownups as well as the children carried them everywhere.
But later on, when there seemed to be no danger, the
grownups left theirs at home. Once the bombing finally
started, everyone carried them again.

1940

Rationing Begins

In September 1939 each person received a ration coupon book, but no food or clothes were rationed for a while. However, many things were in short supply for everyday people. The needs of the soldiers came first. Rationing was a way of dividing up what was available as fairly as possible. This meant each family could purchase only a certain amount of a particular item each month, and it wasn't a very big amount. You paid for each item with coupons from your ration book as well as money.

Rationing was a terrible hardship for everyone. In November 1939 bacon and butter were rationed. It was one thing to give up luxuries, but people were upset to lose such basic and favorite foods. Like all the other families that we knew, we ate bacon and eggs for breakfast every morning. There was always butter for every meal, too. It took us a long time to get used to having just toast and margarine for breakfast. At first we sometimes had a boiled egg, but after a while there were no fresh eggs either. We had to use powdered eggs instead.

By January 1940 many things were rationed, including clothes and petrol (gasoline). As the months passed, the list of rationed items grew longer and longer, although bread, potatoes, vegetables, fruit, and fish were never rationed. However, some were in short supply from time to time. Bananas and oranges, for example, were rarely available.

Each family had to choose one grocery shop and register with it. You weren't allowed to buy groceries anywhere else. Mum didn't mind too much about the rationing. Some foods just weren't available any more, and she knew that the soldiers needed the best food so that they would stay strong and healthy. But she often grumbled, as did everyone else, about how the rich people seemed to get whatever they wanted. She read in the newspaper that wealthy ladies were buying huge supplies of sugar in case it was rationed later on.

I'll never forget the number on my ration book: ODIJ 2293. Its cover was cream-colored. I spent hours clutching it and hoping that, magically, enough coupons would appear in it so that I could get some new shoes. But they never did! From time to time, someone came to school to measure our feet. If only my feet would grow to longer than nine inches, I would be given ration coupons for the new shoes that I longed for and desperately needed. Throughout the war, I ate potatoes until I thought I would burst, trying to grow longer feet. Unfortunately, they never quite reached the required length. I had unusually wide feet and was stuck with miserably uncomfortable, ill-fitting hand-me-downs until after the war.

Even though food was in short supply, on April 27, 1940, my fifth birthday, Mum somehow managed to gather enough extra food for me to have a birthday party. Eight of my friends were invited. We played lots of games and then sat down to eat. There were all kinds of sandwiches, and Mum had made a beautiful snow scene as a centerpiece for the table. On top of a large block of salt was a small igloo carved out of more salt, a toy sled, and five tiny trees. I thought it was beautiful. One of my friends sat with her hands in her lap and ate nothing. When Mum asked her why, she said, "I'm waiting for you to cut the birthday cake." She burst into tears when Mum explained to her that it wasn't a real cake.

1940

Royalty Comes to Lydney

By April 1940 the war on the continent of Europe was becoming much worse. The months that had been called the "Phoney War" and "This Strangest of Wars" were over. Hitler was invading country after country. He had taken over Norway and Denmark and was now attacking Holland, Belgium, and France. British soldiers were fighting everywhere, trying hard to help their European allies. But the Nazis kept advancing further and further forward, and no one seemed able to stop them.

On April 13 at 5:00 A.M., King George received a phone call from Queen Wilhelmina of Holland, asking for assistance for her country and her family. By the end of that day, Queen Wilhelmina, her daughter Juliana, and Juliana's husband, Prince Bernhard, were living in Lydney. Lord Bledisloe was allowing the Dutch royal family to share his mansion just across the fields from my house. A private school that had been evacuated from near London was already using his other, much larger home, on the same estate.

Lord Bledisloe was quite old when Queen Wilhelmina came to live in Lydney. He had been Governor-General of New Zealand for a great many years. He was much-loved in New Zealand and an important man in the British government's House of Lords. I had once seen Queen Mary, the mother of King George, when she came to stay with Lord Bledisloe. She arrived in a horse-drawn carriage wearing a diamond tiara and a long blue dress.

My friend Janet Windsor's father was assigned to be Prince Bernhard's nighttime bodyguard as part of his Home Guard duties. The Home Guard was a little like the A.R.P. that my dad belonged to, except that the two groups divided up the duties. Every town had a Home Guard, and my dad was part of that, too. The Home Guard was like an army of local people who were not soldiers. Later, it became known all over Britain as "Dad's Army."

Janet's dad was stationed outside the prince's bedroom door, and around midnight each night, Prince Bernhard climbed through the window to go for a spin in his little red sports car. Since he wasn't allowed to use his car's headlights, this was very dangerous. Janet's dad soon asked to be relieved of his duty. The anxiety of guarding the prince was too much responsibility for him!

Every Sunday morning for a while we saw Queen Wilhelmina and her family in our church. She sat in the front pew with Lord Bledisloe and his wife. At the end of the service she stood outside the church door shaking hands with the churchgoers as they left. I was not impressed! I thought that queens were supposed to have crowns on their heads and wear beautiful gowns like Queen Mary. Queen Wilhelmina wore drab clothes and looked just like everyone else. Before long, she moved to London, and her daughter went to Canada.

1940

The Little Ships

In May 1940 news came that over three hundred thousand French and British soldiers were trapped near the town of Dunkirk on the coast of France, a few miles from the Belgian border. The Nazis had them surrounded, and it seemed as if they would all be killed or taken prisoner. The only way they could be rescued was to be taken by boat across the English Channel to England. On May 26 the naval evacuation of the soldiers from Dunkirk began. Three days later, most of the men were still waiting to be rescued. There simply weren't enough ships available.

All the yacht clubs in the southern part of England were contacted by wireless and telephone. Yacht owners were told to stand ready. On May 29 on the 1:00 P.M. news, a broadcast went out asking for every small seaworthy pleasure craft, fishing boat, or freighter to report immediately to the Admiralty at Dover on the southeast coast of England.

They were to take part in what was called "Operation Dynamo." They were told nothing else.

Clem Gardener of Lydney had, until recently, owned a boat named the *Princess Pat*, a small converted lifeboat. She was different from most boats because she was powered by a car engine. Mr. Gardener had sold her to a man who lived on the southern coast of England. The new owner phoned Mr. Gardener and told him that he and the *Princess Pat* were to be in Dover by May 31. He had no idea what he would be asked to do, but if it would help win the war, then he wanted to be a part of it.

The new owner told Mr. Gardener that when word had spread around his town that he needed petrol for the trip to Dover, people came forward bringing whatever they could spare. Soon he had all that he needed. They gave him extra food and blankets, too. The government had ordered each sailor to carry three days' worth of rations.

Mr. Gardener felt very proud when he heard the news. He had owned the *Princess Pat* for many years and had done a lot of work to make her a seaworthy, powerful boat. He told everyone he met that the *Princess Pat* was going to take part in the war. Mum and I thought that the new owner was very brave. We could tell that Mr. Gardener wished that he still owned the boat and could be part of the rescue mission.

The *Princess Pat* was one of a thousand little ships that

answered the call for help. At 2:30 P.M. on Friday, May 31, the first of the little ships left Dover to begin a 55-mile northeasterly journey across the English Channel to Dunkirk. It was the middle of the night before the last of the boats set off. Some went by an even more northerly 87-mile route, while others went south from Dover and sailed a 39-mile route. The shorter, 26-mile route straight across the Channel was filled with mines (which are like floating bombs) planted there by the German navy. The procession took the longer routes in order to get to Dunkirk safely.

No one had any idea what they would find when they got to Dunkirk. For once, the always-gray water of the Channel was calm, yet a heavy cloud cover hung overhead, usually a sign of stormy weather. It was dark and very gloomy, but even the boats that traveled at night could not use their lights for fear of being seen by Nazi patrols. Miraculously, the enemy had stopped their incessant bombing of ships crossing the Channel. All was quiet.

On the beaches of Dunkirk the thousands of Allied soldiers who were trapped at the coast feared they had been abandoned. But that Friday afternoon the tired, dirty, exhausted, and frightened soldiers saw an incredible sight. Over one thousand small ships appeared on the horizon: sailboats, paddle steamers, barges, lifeboats, cargo ships, motorboats, car ferries, naval vessels, and small freighters were approaching the shore. Some were pulling others that had run out of petrol. The *Princess Pat,* originally from Lydney, was sailing proudly among them.

At home in Lydney we were all listening anxiously to every broadcast and praying for the *Princess Pat.* Word had spread that she had once belonged to Mr. Gardener, and we had adopted her as our own. The adventure was almost over before we began to understand where the little boat had gone.

Dunkirk has a 15-foot tide, so at low tide, the water is shallow for a very long way out. Because of this, naval ships couldn't get close enough to the beaches to rescue anyone. And there wasn't room for many of them to tie up at the long piers that jutted far out into the deeper water. Most of the smaller boats were being used at Dunkirk and neighboring La Panne to ferry men from the beaches out to the larger ships. Back and forth, back and forth they went, each time carrying more and more men to safety. Everyone worked as fast as possible. They knew that the Germans would reach Dunkirk soon.

All types of people were sailing the little ships. Articles in the newspapers described bankers still in their smart city suits and bowler hats, farmers, teachers, doctors, dentists, and fishermen. Many of the captains had only sailed on calm rivers or around harbors before, and never in the sea. No one had taken the time to change into waterproof sailing clothes. One of the paddle steamers that came from near

Lydney hadn't been to sea since the 1890s! The larger rescue boats carried soldiers from Dunkirk all the way across the Channel and back to England. No matter how tired the captains were, as soon as their ships were unloaded and re-fuelled in Dover, they set off again across the Channel. Some of the rescue boats returned to Dunkirk as many as a dozen times.

In early June, when the *Princess Pat* sailed proudly back into her home port, dozens of people were there to meet her. She had taken part in what the newspapers said was the greatest rescue in history. J. B. Priestly, a famous English journalist, said in a radio broadcast that future generations of British children would learn "how the little holiday steamers made an excursion to hell and came back glorious."

The new owner of the *Princess Pat* wrote to Mr. Gardener immediately, telling him about the soldiers he had saved and how terrifying it had been to see Dunkirk in flames as he sailed closer and closer to the shore. On the return journey, there was so much water in the boat and so many men that he feared she would sink, but she didn't. The *Princess Pat* had done well. When Mr. Gardener read the letter to us, he made us feel as if we had all been part of an incredible adventure. Most of us cried as we listened.

The rescues at Dunkirk continued from May 26 until early on the morning of June 4, 1940. The wireless said that, with the help of the little ships, 338,226 men were saved, of which 225,000 were British and the rest were French soldiers. The little ships also rescued a goose and a lot of frightened, abandoned dogs and puppies. The evacuation was a tremendous success.

We were sad to hear that at 4:00 A.M. on June 4, when the last of the rescues were made, some of the wounded soldiers had to be left behind. Throughout the evacuation, the wounded had been kept at Château Rosendael, a castle in the town of Dunkirk. There they could be comfortable and continue to receive medical care. As many as possible of the walking wounded had been taken to the rescue boats every day, but when the last boats arrived, only those who could walk unaided were able to make the journey to the beach. The German army was getting closer and closer, and speed was vital. Many wounded soldiers were captured and became Nazi prisoners of war.

It was 9:00 A.M. on the morning of June 4 when the German army finally entered Dunkirk. The forty thousand Frenchmen who had held out against the Nazis to ensure the safety of those who escaped finally surrendered. A batallion of seven thousand British soldiers had also fought bravely on the outskirts of the town so that the evacuation could be carried out successfully. All were taken prisoner. Already, more than a million Dutch, British, Belgian, and French prisoners had been captured in the area as the Nazis pushed the Allied army closer and closer to the coast. The town and beaches were littered with British and French guns, tanks, and jeeps that had been left behind. For Hitler, it was a great victory.

Over two hundred of the little ships were sunk. Some of the volunteer sailors and their passengers died, but many were rescued by other ships. The battle at Dunkirk was considered to be a major military defeat for the Allies. However, the British people hailed "Operation Dynamo" as a victory. Much to the surprise of the soldiers, they were welcomed back as heroes. The British were overjoyed that most of the ships and soldiers had arrived home safely and very proud of the brave volunteers who made the rescue possible.

1940

The Stay-at-Home Dads

My father didn't go to war. He was part of the Home Guard as well as the A.R.P. Because Dad was a chemistry teacher, the government wanted him to continue teaching rather than going off to fight in the war. He was training young scientists, and they would be needed if the war continued much longer.

As a scientist, Dad also had a second job. He was trained as a poison gas lecturer, and he became the expert in our area. As Gas Officer, he traveled many miles by bus or bicycle in the evenings, giving lectures in towns and villages about how to survive a gas attack. Everyone was certain that Hitler would drop poisonous gas bombs sooner or later, and we had to be prepared.

I always felt guilty that my father wasn't somewhere fighting bravely, as most of my friends' fathers were doing. My best friend Jill's dad was in India, and my godfather was in North Africa. To a child it all sounded very exotic and not at all dangerous, although it was. We heard about the husbands and sons of neighbors getting killed every day.

After a while, those of us with stay-at-home dads began to realize that they had important work to do, too. They did their regular jobs during the day and their A.R.P. or Home Guard duties in the evening. Every night they kept a lookout for German fighter planes in the skies overhead, and they always had to enforce the blackout.

Often at night we saw the Nazi planes flying low as they followed the nearby Severn River on their way to Birmingham. The drone of their engines was a chilling sound. I was terrified whenever I heard it. The silvery river shone in the moonlight, making it easy for the planes to find their way to their target. Sometimes we heard the sound of gunfire from across the river as British soldiers tried to shoot the planes down.

The Home Guard was a volunteer army that had about six guns for every one hundred men. The few guns the farmers owned had been collected for the war effort long before. The Home Guard had to train with brooms and spears, and they felt really foolish. Only a few men had uniforms. As time went on, they became more organized, but the nights were very long for them. Every shadow began to look like a Nazi soldier. If a German plane crashed, the Home Guard volunteers had to capture any airmen who were still alive. It could be a dangerous task.

One night a German parachutist landed in the field next to our house. His plane had crashed somewhere nearby. We watched my dad through the window as he walked across the field to talk to the soldier. We were terrified as we wondered what would happen. Perhaps the German would attack my dad, or even shoot him. We were too scared to go outside and see what was happening.

It was a very long time until my dad came back. Luckily, the soldier wasn't hurt, and he didn't have a gun. My father had to escort him to the Home Guard office, and from there he was taken to a prisoner-of-war camp. When Dad came home, he told us all about it. The prisoner didn't speak any English, but Dad told us that he was only about eighteen years old and seemed like a nice lad, just like the boys that he taught at school. My dad said he couldn't imagine that such a nice young boy was our enemy. As we talked, we realized that a great many of the German people were probably just like us. Perhaps they didn't want the war either.

In London and Birmingham, where the bombing was the worst, the main responsibility of the A.R.P. and the Home Guard was to rescue people who were buried alive when bombs landed directly on their homes. Or they gave medical care. Or drove people to the hospital. Or dug out dogs and other pets that were buried in the rubble.

My Uncle Fred didn't go to war either. Because he was very clever with his hands, he was assigned to the job of

building and maintaining aircraft. Uncle Fred wanted so
badly to pilot a Spitfire, one of the tiny planes that were
doing so much damage to the *Luftwaffe*, the German air-
force. But he was never allowed to learn to fly.

In August 1939, Mum and Dad rented a small bungalow in a coastal town two hours by train from Lydney. The weather was perfect, and the possibility of war was forgotten. It would be our last holiday for many years.

GOVERNMENT EVACUATION SCHEME

The Government have ordered evacuation of school children.

If your children are registered for evacuation send them to their assembly point at once.

If your children are not registered and you wish them to be evacuated, the teachers or the school keeper will help you.

If you do not wish your children to be evacuated you must not send them to school until further notice.

Posters notifying the arrival of parties in the country will be displayed at the schools at which the children assembled for evacuation.

After war was declared, my cousin Audrey was evacuated from Birmingham. I was thrilled to have tea parties with this new live-in friend. The bombing had not yet started. *Left:* In September 1939, the government advised that all children and mothers with babies should leave London immediately. Posters appeared everywhere. Many of them showed young children ready to leave London. *Courtesy of The Imperial War Museum, London.*

Being an evacuee was bewildering and often frightening. Parents thought they'd never see their children again, and children felt abandoned. With address labels around their necks, and gas masks in boxes, most children had no idea where they were going. *Courtesy of The Imperial War Museum, London.*

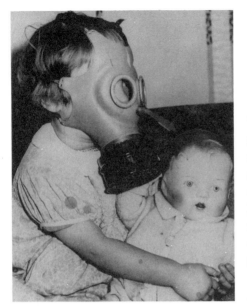

This small girl is wearing a gas mask designed for toddlers. My own mask was brown and black, and smelled awful. *Below:* An Anderson shelter three miles from my home. The vines growing across it made it invisible. Even in the countryside, families felt the need for a safe place to hide. *Courtesy of The Imperial War Museum, London.*

Many small craft, like these on the River Thames, were towed home across the English Channel during the evacuation of Dunkirk. Some of them had run out of petrol. All of them, both big and small, carried soldiers back to England. *Courtesy of The Imperial War Museum, London.*

At night, during the air raids, a great many Londoners slept in the underground railway tunnels. Since the trains stopped running at night, people often slept between the tracks. In some stations, W.V.S. ladies served tea and hot meals. *Courtesy of The Imperial War Museum, London.*

1940

Bombing and Tea-Rationing

Living in the country as we did, we were able to pretend that nothing much had changed. It was true that more and more foods were being rationed, our clothes were wearing out, and that most of the men had gone to war. But, for a while, things seemed almost normal.

Then two major disasters occurred. On June 18, 1940, the Nazi s began nightly bombing raids. Some attacks involved only a few bombers and were described as "light" raids. London was the main target. When the heavy bombing started, Londoners referred to it as "The Blitz " — from the German word *Blitzkrieg*, "lightning war." This term was used to describe the sudden attacks. The bombers flew in swiftly and unexpectedly, dropped their bombs, and then disappeared as quickly as they'd come. They had to act quickly because at that time German planes were barely able to carry enough fuel for the return flight home.

Often there was no time to sound the air raid siren.

People weren't able to get to the safety of the bomb shelters or down into "the Tube," the underground train tunnels, where thousands of Londoners hid night after night during the war. Although the attack was over quickly, the results were devastating. Many people were killed, and a lot of damage was done to the city.

The second blow fell on July 9, when tea was rationed. The British people love their tea. They drink it with every meal and several times between each meal. Nothing could have been worse for British morale than a shortage of tea. It was all anyone seemed to talk about. My mother loved to take a break from her housework and sit down with "a nice cup of tea." She couldn't imagine not being able to do that.

But while the people of Lydney were grumbling about tea-rationing, Londoners were being bombed and bombed. In July, the bombing raids became much heavier, and on July 10, the Royal Air Force engaged the Nazi planes in the first air battle over British soil. The wireless called it "The Battle of Britain."

During 1940 the war began to heat up even more, and a great many more men and boys were recruited into the army, navy, and air force. An eighteen-year-old neighbor who had joined the army wrote home that they had to drill with broomsticks because no guns were available. There was no doubt about it. Britain was not ready to defend herself from an invasion by the "Jerries," as we called the Nazis.

Hitler thought that Britain would surrender now, since

she had a poorly trained army and all her allies had been defeated. Mum and Dad tried to explain to me that every country in Europe that had been a friend to Great Britain was now occupied by German soldiers. We'd heard that the Nazis were behaving with great cruelty in all of the countries that they occupied. Britain was going to have to fight the war alone. Mum and Dad seemed more worried than ever.

Then, all over Britain, German bombers dropped thousands of copies of a speech by Hitler. Its title was "The Last Appeal to Reason." The pamphlet tried to convince the British people that their situation was hopeless and they should surrender. Britain chose to ignore it, so Hitler announced that on August 13, the German *Luftwaffe* would destroy the British Royal Air Force.

But it didn't happen.

1940

The Spitfire Funds

In August 1940 Mum read me an article from the newspaper about something called the "Spitfire Funds." A schoolboy had sent Lord Beaverbrook, who was the owner of several newspapers, one guinea (an English gold coin no longer in circulation) to pay for a thermometer for a Spitfire. The Spitfires were small, one-person British planes that fought bravely against the much larger German bombers. Lord Beaverbrook wrote about the boy in his newspapers, praising him for his generous gift.

In those days a guinea could buy a great deal and was a large contribution for a schoolboy to make. For example, in 1940 one guinea would have bought forty-two four-ounce bars of chocolate, sixty-three pounds of sugar, or almost eight gallons of milk! Today a guinea (worth about $1.68 at the current rate of exchange) would buy very little—perhaps one gallon of milk on sale. But what a difference that boy's donation made to the war effort! His idea caught on, and the number of donations grew and grew.

When they read about the boy's donation in the London newspaper, a Jamaican newspaper telephoned Lord Beaverbrook to ask how much a Hurricane bomber would cost. Jamaica was then a British Crown colony and wanted to do its part for the war. They were told that the price was £20,000 (pounds sterling). Within a week the money had arrived in England. At that time, an average-priced terraced house in London (one attached in a row) sold for £800. The price of one Hurricane bomber would have bought *twenty-five* of these houses—the equivalent of around $2 million at today's prices! Money began to arrive from all over the world from one person, a group, or an entire city.

Before long, at the end of every wireless broadcast by the British Broadcasting Corporation, or the "B.B.C.," as it is called, the list of Spitfire donations was read. For those who wanted to know exactly where their money was going, a price list of component parts was issued. For example, 6 pence (the price of a chocolate bar) bought a rivet, £22 (almost a month's salary for a teacher in 1940) bought a small bomb, and £2,000 bought an airplane wing. By April of 1941 over £13 million ($20.8 million) had been donated, which was an incredible amount of money then. Almost every big town had its name on a Spitfire, and a few had their names on Hurricane bombers.

Oh, how I wished I were old enough to have pocket money! I wanted to pay for part of a Spitfire, too. Whenever I saw one, I thought about how brave the pilot must be to hurtle toward the enemy in such a tiny plane.

1940

The War Comes Closer

Before dark each evening, we laid our clothes out for the next morning. We never knew what each night would bring. Most of our evenings, and many of the nights, too, we spent hiding in the cloakroom (closet) under the stairs, while the German bombers flew low overhead. Our tiny coat cupboard had been reinforced with piles of bricks and was the strongest, safest place in the house.

The moment we heard the scream of the air raid siren, under the stairs we went, sometimes in our pajamas and dressing gowns (robes). Often we'd hurriedly change into the warm clothes we had laid out earlier since we never knew how many hours we'd huddle there. We spent as much time crowded under the stairs waiting for the "All Clear" signal as we did in our own cozy beds.

Sometimes we read or played games while we waited. There really wasn't enough room to lie down and sleep, but we napped a little, leaning on each other. And always, our ears were alerted for the drone of the German bombers as they followed the Severn River, just a mile from our house, all the way to Birmingham. After what seemed like an eternity, the long-awaited "All Clear" wailed across the rooftops, and we would stumble sleepily upstairs to bed.

Lydney was lucky to survive the war with no damage. The nightly parade of German planes flying to the Midlands seemed unending. The Nazi pilots followed the landmarks below to guide them to their targets, so lakes had been drained to confuse them. But no one could hide the wide silver river, especially on moonlit nights when the water shone like a bright, metallic ribbon. After dark, the river became a sinister place. It made Birmingham and the rest of the Midlands easy to find, or a "sitting duck" for the bombers, as my parents often said. We had no telephone, so there was never any quick way to find out if all of our many relatives there were still alive after each bomb attack. However, since no one was actually killed in Lydney, I could never imagine anyone else we knew dying, no matter where in England they lived.

My family lived at the top of a hill in the last house on the street. Attached to our garden wall was a huge searchlight that faced the Severn River. Every night "our" beam came on automatically at dusk and circled and circled, throwing its light high into the sky above the river. I was always afraid that it would draw attention to our house and that a "Jerry" bomber would drop a bomb directly on us. But that never happened.

Somewhere, not too far away, someone must have had the job of watching "our" beam, just in case an enemy plane crossed its path. And somewhere, there must have been at least one anti-aircraft gun, ready to fire on that enemy plane. Perhaps the searchlights were there in case the radar broke down. No matter what the reason, they circled endlessly in a giant arc, night after night.

Radar was invented in Britain in 1935. It was called "radio location" at first, but in 1943, scientists in the United States who had been working to further develop it changed the name to "radar," for "radio detection and ranging." It served as a type of early warning system and could detect the approach of enemy planes or ships when they were still a great distance away in daylight or darkness, fog, or rain. The Nazis did not have radar, or even anything similar, so its invention was a tremendous advantage for Britain.

During one of our visits to Birmingham, we found the ground littered with long strips of tinfoil. The Germans had dropped it by the ton to confuse British radar. Never mind what its original purpose was. We children though it was the best present we had had in a long time. We gathered up masses of it and took it back to Lydney, where we made it into wonderful Christmas decorations! Whether in some way the foil helped the Nazis in their bombing raids on Birmingham, we never knew.

On November 14, 1940, Coventry, a large city in the Midlands near Birmingham, was destroyed by German bombers. Just ten days later, from our front garden we watched the devastation of the city of Bristol, only 19 miles away from us. The Severn River is 3 miles wide at Bristol, and on that night the entire river appeared to be lit by flames.

As the bombing of Bristol began, bonfires were lit on every uninhabited hillside for miles around. The hope was that the German pilots would be confused about the exact location of Bristol and drop their bombs near the bonfires. It was an amazing sight, but the trick failed. The wireless called the attack the "Coventration" of Bristol because Bristol was destroyed just as Coventry had been. Bristol's Lord Mayor spoke on the wireless and said that the bombing was like a "volcanic cataclysm." Being only five at the time, I didn't understand the words, but I have never forgotten what I saw that night. It wasn't hard for even a child to imagine what he meant.

After that, a broken-down cargo ship was anchored in the Severn River. Night after night it was set on fire to divert some of the German bombers to that spot. People hoped that the German *Luftwaffe* would mistakenly think the burning ship was the heart of Bristol and dump their bombs in the river instead of on the city.

1940-41

Mums and Children Get Involved

On the "Home Front," as it was called, women had become much more involved in the war effort. Many of the Lydney women worked in factories, some of them making aircraft parts. It was found that women, their small fingers made nimble by years of knitting and sewing, were much better than the men at working with small parts. They were even better at welding!

Other women set up small factories in their own homes. They, too, made airplane parts and other things needed to fight the war, but since they had small children at home, they couldn't work in the large factories. After the work day, many of them spent long hours on the factory roofs, working as plane spotters. Whenever they saw planes approaching, they informed the local army post so that action could be taken.

Some young women became farm workers and were called "Land Girls." But the farmers complained that they needed three girls to do the work of two men. Families began to take working vacations on farms. They didn't earn anything, but since the farmer fed them and gave them a place to stay, it was a cheap way to have a peaceful (but hard-working) holiday in the country and help the war effort at the same time. We saw families of strangers in the shops in Lydney whenever the crops were ready to be picked.

My mother joined something called the "Women's Voluntary Service" (W.V.S). Because I was only five, she didn't have to become a factory worker, but there were other things that she could do to help. In Lydney most of the W.V.S. mums spent their days darning socks for the soldiers (nothing could be thrown away) or knitting scarves, socks, and woolen caps called "balaclavas." The balaclavas were first worn by British soldiers during the Crimean War in 1854. The Battle of Balaclava was fought in a part of Russia known as the Crimea. Balaclava was the major port in the area, and the caps were named after the port. Looking a little like ski masks, they covered the whole head, neck, and ears. It was important that our soldiers fighting in Europe during the frozen winter months be kept as warm as possible.

Lydney's W.V.S., like most of the groups, had a mobile canteen. It was a large van with a kitchen inside. When a troop train or lorries (trucks) bulging with soldiers passed through Lydney or stopped at the railway station in town, the W.V.S. ladies were always there in their van serving gallons of tea and hot meals to the men. Often at night convoys of lorries filled with soldiers rumbled through the town. Then the W.V.S. would be on a duty in the town hall at midnight providing hot meals and hot tea. The W.V.S. fed the women working in the factories, too. They even organized a bicycle relay service so that if the telephone system were ever destroyed, they could take turns riding across the countryside to inform everyone about what was happening.

Like lots of other British children, I worked to collect reusable scrap metals. It was called "salvage collection." We would go from house to house, asking for things like old saucepans that could be melted down and used to make plane or tank parts. Every house had its iron railings and gates confiscated. Parks, shops, railway stations, and offices were stripped, too. Kitchen waste was collected and fed to pigs. Everything was recycled in those days, including paper. Oddly enough, it was many, many years after the war before people in England started thinking about recycling again.

A lot of boys in Lydney who were between sixteen and eighteen years of age joined the Air Training Corps (A.T.C). The program started at schools all over Britain and was very popular. The boys were given Royal Air Force uniforms and trained to fly and to fight. When they turned eighteen, they went into the Royal Air Force.

Most of the schools had hobby clubs that also helped

the war effort. We children learned such things as pig-keeping, clothes-mending, and vegetable-growing. Some students even made aircraft parts. There were also camps where teenagers from the cities stayed and helped to harvest potatoes, cabbages, and other vegetables.

Everywhere we went we saw huge posters reminding us to "Keep the Home Fires Burning." Mum said it meant that everyone should be ready to welcome husbands and sons and brothers home when the war ended. I sometimes felt that the war would *never* end. I thought the British army, navy, and air force who were fighting so bravely would *never* return home. I'd *never* have new clothes. And food would be rationed *forever*.

1940-41

Preparing for the Nazi Invasion

For me, life during daylight hours was often peaceful, but after dark, the nightmare began again. During the day, Lydney was still a quiet country town of about four thousand people. Along with all of the other children, I went to school every day, rain or shine; the stay-at-home dads went to work; and the mums did their factory work, helped at the W.V.S., and cooked and cleaned and shopped. But now there was a new concern. We began to prepare for a Nazi invasion.

My family, like every other family in Britain, was asked to gather together all the old junk it could find. We were told to scatter it on fields and golf courses so that enemy aircraft, especially the tiny gliders, couldn't land. I thought that the countryside looked awful littered with old cars, beds, prams (baby carriages), chairs, and other rubbish. We even saw barricades being built across main roads. The idea was to make it as difficult as possible for enemy tanks to travel around Britain. The barricades were huge and made up of every kind of junk you could imagine. Old doors, planks, barbed wire, and cement blocks were the most useful contributions. The barricades had to be moved whenever the British tanks and lorries needed to pass through a town. Most conversations I overheard were about how the Nazis would treat us when they invaded our country. We heard more and more terrible rumors about their cruelty. Townspeople all over Europe were killed if they didn't obey orders quickly enough. From time to time, news of the prisoner-of-war camps reached the newspapers. We read interviews with prisoners who had escaped and succeeded in getting back to England. The Nazis were angry at how skilled the British airmen were at maneuvering their tiny planes, so imprisoned airmen were getting very bad treatment. But others were suffering even more at the Nazis' hands.

Hitler had ordered that every Jewish person in Germany and the countries she had invaded was to be imprisoned. Jews who escaped from Germany just as the war was starting told the newspapers that already a great many of their friends and relatives had been put into concentration camps. Every day, more and more Jewish people were being identified and rounded up. It wasn't until the war was over and the Allies liberated the remaining prisoners that we learned with horror about the six million Jews who were tortured and killed in these terrible camps. Hitler had tried to exterminate every Jew during that time, a period that historians now call the "Holocaust."

A few days before the war broke out, a British government organization safely brought ten thousand Jewish children out of Germany, Austria, Czechoslovakia, and Poland. They were taken to England, and safety, on special trains called "*Kindertransport.*" In order to participate, Jewish families had to first apply, then find a sponsor in England, such as a friend or relative. The sponsor paid £10 ($16) and agreed to be responsible for the child when he or she arrived. Some were sponsored by Jewish families, and others went to Christian homes. The children didn't think they would ever see their parents again, so it was a terrifying time for them.

When they heard about the Nazis' cruelty, the British people wondered if they were capable of being cruel themselves. Most planned to escape into the hills and forests far away from the main roads when the Nazis came. Everyone was trying to be brave, but we were all secretly very frightened.

The government was determined to keep any enemy soldiers who landed by parachute from using British vehicles. A special locking device was put on buses to immobilize them when they weren't in use. Our neighbor was taught how to remove the rotor arm from his car so that no one else could drive it. If a car owner didn't do that, policemen had orders to let the air out of the tires and then make the owner pay a heavy fine. Another part of the plan was that petrol stations were to be destroyed when the invasion began. Without fuel, the Nazis wouldn't be able to travel far.

Mum and Dad explained that it wouldn't be as easy for Germany to invade Britain as it had been for them to take over the countries that surrounded them in Europe. We had the English Channel to protect us. Twenty-six miles across at its narrowest point, the Channel was like a giant moat. Germany would need a great many boats to carry enough soldiers and tanks across the Channel. If their invading army were too small, the Germans would have no chance of defeating Britain. They would all be shot as they tried to get through the rolls of barbed wire that lined all of the southern beaches.

Another tactic designed to confuse the Germans worked a little too well. All over Britain, signposts and street names were removed so that the Germans wouldn't be able to find their way around. Suddenly, traveling became a nightmare. Buses no longer showed their destinations. Train stations had no names. The problem was that the British people themselves couldn't find their way around! Neither could the British army. Britain is covered with narrow, twisting, winding roads with high hedgerows. It is very easy to get lost even with signposts, especially around the Forest of Dean, near Lydney, where five roads from one village can lead to the same destination.

After a while, a few signs giving vague directions like "To the Southwest" appeared, to help the British army. In towns close to the southern and eastern coasts, three-inch-high signs were put up, but they were extremely difficult to see even in daylight. Travel after dark was impossible. Everywhere was pitch black.

More and more people gave their houses names so that they would have an identity. For example, our house was called "Four Winds." That way, it was still possible to ask for directions to someone's house even though there were no street names.

1942

Make Do and Mend

In the spring of 1942 clothes-rationing became a much more serious matter. Men and women had been allowed forty-eight coupons a year. Just five months later, it was reduced to thirty-six coupons. With this amount, a man could buy three pairs of socks, one-and-a-half pairs of shoes, one set of underwear, and a pair of trousers in one year; one shirt every twenty months; a jacket every two years; a sweater every five years; and an overcoat every seven years. In order to save fabric, shirt tails were made two inches shorter. No matter what size your feet were, socks could be only nine inches long.

Although it was fashionable for men to have cuffs on their trousers, this was considered a waste of fabric during wartime. And, for the same reason, most of their trousers and jackets were now made without pockets, too. For men, losing trouser cuffs and pockets was a crisis of the same magnitude as tea-rationing was for women. Having fewer pockets had a terrible effect on the morale of the men, so in 1944 the government allowed clothing factories to put the pockets back again!

For women, manufacturers were only allowed to produce six styles of clothing. The size and number of pleats for skirts and dresses, the number of buttonholes, and the width of sleeves were all set by the government. Since the clothes were all alike, women wore the brightest colors they could find. In the factories, colorful head scarves and turbans became the fashion. During the war, women in Britain also wore trousers for the first time ever.

The British women loved to go to the cinema to escape the worries and misery of the war. Two American movie stars, Joan Crawford and Veronica Lake, had become very popular. Every woman in Britain wanted to look like them. So, like Joan, they put huge shoulder pads in their dresses and jackets, and they copied Veronica's wide-brimmed hats that dropped low on one side. Her hairstyle was copied, too. Her hair was long, and it covered one eye before curling under at the ends. Unfortunately, since the British women had to wear ankle socks instead of stockings, being a Veronica Lake or Joan Crawford look-alike was an impossible dream.

In wartime, clothes had to be really old before they were ready to be cut up and remade. For the children, the slogan MAKE DO AND MEND became "our" slogan. Because clothing was now so expensive, and coupons were so few, all of our clothes were made from our parents' old clothes. I'd never noticed until then that my dad wore mostly brown and gray and that my mum liked blue. I suppose I should have been grateful that Mum was an extremely good dressmaker, but I grew to loathe brown, gray, and blue. As beautifully as my mother made my recycled clothes, they still weren't new.

The only change from my homemade clothing was when the W.V.S. ladies exchanged old clothes from their own children. I hated someone else's hand-me-downs even more than I hated re-used material. But at least they weren't always brown, blue, or gray. Teenagers and overweight children got extra coupons for clothes. I began to wonder if I should increase my potato-eating and try to gain weight since my feet wouldn't cooperate and grow long enough to qualify me for new shoes! I'd get extra coupons, which meant new clothes, maybe even *red* ones. Unfortunately, my potato-eating didn't have any effect until the war was long over and I was a teenager—an overweight teenager!

To keep children warm, an undershirt known as a "liberty bodice" was developed. It was white, very thick, and had heavy ridges running up and down it. It looked and felt like the old-fashioned corsets that many women still wore. In a country without central heating in most homes, houses were drafty and often cold. The liberty bodices kept us warm and hopefully reduced the number of colds we had. But I doubt if they were any thinner than the bullet-proof vests that policemen wear now. It might even have been bullet proof! Luckily, I never had to put it to the test.

Toward the end of the war, we wore something that was even worse than the liberty bodice. White parachute silk became available for making underwear. Parachutes are made from incredibly long, narrow triangles of fabric. Our mums used the silk to make us petticoats because our dresses were worn so thin. But within minutes of putting the slip on and starting to walk, the fabric would spiral tightly around our legs and make it impossible to move.

And then there was the ballet dress I was forced to perform in at local concerts. The dress was made from something called "butter muslin," which was similar to bandage material. The knickers (panties), which traditionally have most of the tutu's frills on them, were trimmed with strips of three-inch-wide gathered bandages. They were so heavy that by the end of every dance, they had dropped to my knees. Sometimes they'd dropped all the way to my ankles! Despite the embarrassment, I never gave up my dream of becoming a professional ballet dancer when I grew up.

1942

Special Treats

On November 9, 1942, my baby sister, Margaret Faith (Fay), was born. It would be a long time before she'd be old enough to play with me, so I was not very impressed. Baby equipment, like everything else, was in short supply because of the war. My sister slept in a cradle made out of a cardboard box. And every evening she was enclosed in her gas mask for a while. She needed to learn not to be frightened by it.

The best thing about having a baby sister was the Ministry of Food orange juice. It was a thick, syrupy substance that was orange in color but not in taste. Still, it was a welcome treat. A baby in the house also meant extra powdered eggs. They were delicious. Along with powdered chocolate, all kinds of good things could be made with them, such as chocolate Rice Krispie squares. In my house we hadn't had treats like that for what seemed like my whole lifetime. And because of the new baby, our family was given a "Family

Allowance"—extra money for feeding the baby. Mum was very happy about that.

As far as food went, one of the greatest moments of my life was having tea at the dentist's house. His daughter, Bridget, was one of my friends. There I ate so many things that we rarely saw, like fresh eggs and butter. I can still taste the fabulous cakes that Bridget's mother made! Dentists, doctors, and shopkeepers always seemed to have more food and much better food than the rest of us. We guessed that they traded their services for rationed foods, but it didn't seem fair. For example, a farmer might pay for a doctor's visit partly with butter and eggs and partly with money. There was also something called the "Black Market." People who could afford it paid high prices to illegally obtain more than their share of the rationed foods.

The rest of us had to put up with the "National Wheatmeal Loaf," which was barely edible. Whenever someone got sick, they blamed it on the bread! One lady had to pay a fine because she wasted the bread by feeding it to the birds. According to our ration books, we were allowed two ounces of butter, four ounces of sugar, and one quarter-pound of meat per person *each week*. However, these things weren't always available at the grocery stores.

No one ever knew what kind of meat they were eating, though most people said it was horse meat. From old horses. Since I wasn't sure what it was, I stopped eating meat. Even when we started to get tinned SPAM from

America, I still wouldn't eat meat. In fact, I did not eat meat again until I was eighteen. During the war I lived on bread and potatoes and not much else.

The Windsors, a family who were friends of ours, were some of the lucky ones. They had distant relatives in Australia. Family in America, Canada, New Zealand, or Australia—even distant relatives—usually meant food parcels. And food parcels meant "treats," often foods that we hadn't seen in England for years.

One Christmas the Windsors received a food parcel from Australia. They opened it excitedly and found all the ingredients for a traditional, rich, dark English Christmas cake. There were packets of flour, nuts, and what looked like mixed dried fruits. Mrs. Windsor baked it, and Mr. Windsor brought us some. We were delighted, and the cake tasted delicious.

A few months later, a letter followed the parcel. We were at their house when the letter arrived, so the Windsors read it aloud to us. It said, "We forgot to tell you that some of Auntie's ashes were in the parcel. She was born in England and wanted the ashes sent back to England for burial. Hope you found them." Their Auntie had died some months before, and her body had been cremated. In an instant we realized what had happened. Her ashes had been mistaken for dried fruits and had been baked into the cake! And we had *eaten* them! It was too late for us to be sick, but we weren't so eager to dig into cake after that!

1942-43

Dig for Victory

In 1940 we began to hear more about a goverment campaign called "Dig for Victory," and by 1942 the program was well established. The idea was that everyone should grow their own fresh vegetables. They could then have a better diet, which would help them stay strong and healthy. The healthier everyone was, the better chance Britain felt it had of winning the war. Our family had one of the largest back gardens (backyards) in the town, so we shared it with the local doctor.

I loved it when Dr. Brambell came on Saturday afternoons to weed his "Victory Garden." His vegetables were planted in neat rows, and tiny signs attached to sticks told the name of each one. On Saturdays I waited patiently for him at the back door because he always played with me when he was ready to leave. He was especially good at playing with tops. He taught me how to use a whip to keep the top spinning for a long time and how to put colored chalk circles on it. As you whipped the top with a long string attached to a stick, it spun faster and faster, and the chalk made wonderful rainbows of color. Our house was at the top of a hill, and our driveway had to be one of the coldest spots on Earth. But I wouldn't have missed playing with Dr. Brambell for anything!

Families who didn't have a big garden like ours, or couldn't find one to share, were given a small strip of land on an empty lot. These strips were called "allotments." Many people kept hens and even pigs on their tiny bits of land. Every house had a bucket in the kitchen for things like potato peelings and other vegetable scraps. Mr. Priest, who lived in a farm cottage near us, collected our scraps to feed to the pig he kept in his tiny garden. He had hens, too, and once in a while, he'd give us some eggs in exchange for the vegetable scraps. What a treat that was! We hardly ever saw a real egg in those days.

Even though every inch of the back gardens was filled with tidy rows of vegetables, all of the front gardens in my town still had neat lawns and an abundance of many kinds of flowers. Mum said these front gardens were an English tradition, and war or no war, that would never change.

"LET US
GO FORWARD
TOGETHER"

Posters of Prime Minister Winston Churchill appeared everywhere.
He was a great leader, and his words filled everyone with courage.
Courtesy of The Imperial War Museum, London.

Our daytime view of the Severn River filled us with peace. At night, the river became a sinister place, its shining silver surface guiding enemy aircraft towards Birmingham. *Below:* The sign on this shop proclaiming BOMBED BUT NOT BEATEN, and the huge Union Jack planted in the rubble, are typical of the attitude of Londoners during the war. *Courtesy of The Imperial War Museum, London.*

Often large, empty buildings became training centers, preparing women for factory work while the men were at war. These ladies are learning to make the tail component of an aircraft. *Courtesy of The Imperial War Museum, London.*

Posters constantly reminded people not to discuss the war where they could be overheard. Even your neighbor could be a spy! Information passed to the Germans about factory locations and products could be disastrous. *Right:* Posters encouraged families to grow vegetables to keep strong and healthy. Healthy people would not surrender! *Courtesy of The Imperial War Museum, London.*

During the war, prisoners of war working on English farms were a familiar sight. Farmers were delighted to once again have men to help them with the heavy work. *Courtesy of The Imperial War Museum, London.*

It would be a long while before she could be my playmate, but with the birth of my sister, Fay, in November 1942, came orange juice, an increased ration of powdered eggs, and more money for my family.

King George and Queen Elizabeth, always concerned and supportive of their subjects, often visited families in areas like the East End of London where bomb damage was the heaviest. *Courtesy of The Imperial War Museum, London.*

When the Yanks arrived, our beautiful Forest of Dean suddenly became the hiding place for American tanks, trucks, guns, bombs and soldiers— but we did not know this until the war was over. *Courtesy of The Imperial War Museum, London.*

1943

Changes at Home

One of the unexpected effects of the war was that it made everyone much friendlier. Mum said that the newspapers were calling it a "bizarre phenomenon." In buses, trains, pubs, shops, and on the street, strangers were speaking to one another. Before the war, that hardly ever happened. It felt wonderful to me. I enjoyed chattering to people on train journeys and in the shops, but before the war they had always looked strangely at me when I tried to start a conversation.

We really noticed how much things had changed when we went to visit my grandparents on the train every few months. In the past, everyone in the compartment would hide their faces behind their newspapers. If I giggled or spoke, all of the newspapers would be lowered a bit. Disapproving eyes would stare over the tops of the newspapers, but no one would speak. Then up would go the newspaper masks again.

During the war, trains didn't run as often, which meant they were always crowded. The train cars each had seats for eight, so it became a wonderful game to see how many people could be squeezed into a compartment. Twenty-eight was usually the maximum, with most of them standing. What a squash it was! It was impossible for anyone to read a newspaper now, and absolutely impossible for such a closely packed group of people not to talk or perhaps even laugh together. If the train stopped suddenly, everyone would fall, and it took ages to untangle the mass of bodies. I loved it!

In the summer of 1943 we got a new kitchen tablecloth. It was made of a new kind of fabric called "American cloth." American cloth was a little like vinyl, except that it had a stringy fabric backing. It could be wiped off with a damp cloth instead of being washed. My baby sister had begun to crawl about that time. Many of our floors were uncarpeted tile or wood, and very cold, so she needed some kind of shoes. Mum cut off pieces of the tablecloth to make slippers for her. She crawled so much that in only a few hours, she had worn the toes out completely. Since she needed a new pair of slippers every day, the shiny new cloth grew smaller and smaller. Soon it was all gone. Fay's first real shoes had wooden soles and cardboard tops. They were awful. I decided that at least hand-me-downs were better than cardboard shoes.

If you needed any new dishes during the war, there was

almost no choice of style. All of them were white. Most cups had no handles. And you could only buy new furniture if your house had been bombed. We never lost our home and still had lots of the pretty flowered dishes that my mum and dad had been given when they got married. A great many other British families were not so lucky.

From time to time one of my classmates arrived at school wearing a black armband over their sleeve. It was a sign of mourning and meant that someone in their family— perhaps their dad or a big brother—had been killed in the war. It was quite a shock to see that black band, and we all became very quiet at the sight of them. Suddenly we were reminded that there really was a war. People were being killed! When your own family was safely around you, it was hard to imagine anything so awful.

1943-45

Prisoners of War

By 1943 Land Girls weren't the only ones working on the local farms. There were large numbers of German prisoners of war, too. Later on, there would be Italians in our area as well. In some parts of England there had been prisoner-of-war camps since 1939.

When the German prisoners arrived, they came straight from the battlefront. Their clothes looked like bloodstained rags. Lydney, as well as the villages in the nearby Forest of Dean, were scoured for old clothes for them to wear and to make into bandages. No one blamed the soldiers for the war. The war was Hitler's fault. I was only eight, but I was sure of that.

After a while, the prisoners were given brown uniforms to wear. On the back were printed the letters "P.W." for "prisoner of war," although they were usually called "P.O.W.s." The German prisoners lived in a village near Lydney; the Italian prisoners were housed in long huts near the river that each held eighty people. The huts were filled with bunks and were crowded and dark.

The Germans were never really treated like prisoners. And no one was afraid of them. Before long they started working on the farms that surrounded Lydney. A lorry would drop them off at the farms where they were most needed early each morning and pick them up again in the evenings. There were no guards. In spring the prisoners planted crops, and in autumn they harvested the crops and dug potatoes. The farmers were delighted to have men working on their farms again.

Some people welcomed the German prisoners into their homes, sharing what food they had and treating them like guests. Some of our neighbors even invited the prisoners to Sunday dinner, always the most important meal of the whole week in England. Our friend, Mrs. Windsor, lived at the opposite end of town from us. She had a lot of prisoners working near her. She went from house to house every day collecting tins of baked beans and soup to heat up and serve to the P.O.W.s.

For a while a prisoner was working in the field close to our house. One day, when Mum could spare a piece of cake and a cigarette, she called out to him. He dropped his spade and ran to the fence as fast as he could. When she handed him the cake, he was in tears, and so was Mum. After that, she gave him food whenever she could.

The British farmers didn't pay the prisoners for their

work. They were prisoners of war, after all. Some of us bought things from the prisoners, such as their watches, to give them a little money to send to their families. We knew that things were bad for women and children in Germany. Money and food were in short supply.

The prisoners were so anxious to earn money that they began to make things to sell. They took sacks apart and colored the threads with dyes made from flowers, leaves, and berries. By braiding the fibers and then stitching the braided ropes together, they made soles for shoes. They begged the women of Lydney for every scrap of material, string, and wool (yarn). And what they got were scraps! The British needed everything usable for themselves. From these minuscule bits of wool the Germans knitted the tops of shoes, attaching them to the braided soles. They also knitted gloves, which they sold for a few pennies. The people of the area were delighted to have shoes to buy. The soles of our shoes had worn out long before, and we had to put torn pieces of cardboard inside our shoes every day to cover the holes.

For one of my birthdays, a friend of my parents bought me a pair of German-knitted gloves. Each finger was different, and there were many different shades of wool knitted into each glove. But the two gloves were identical. They were a little large for me, so I never wore them, but I spent hours looking at them and admiring them.

Italian prisoners came to Lydney in 1944. In their

smart new green uniforms supplied by the American army, they were so different from the soft-spoken Germans who had arrived in rags. The prisoners worked in the local factories, but they had the freedom of the town. Noise and enthusiastic laughter moved through Lydney in waves whenever their shift at the factory ended.

1940–45

Wireless Voices

Winston Churchill was sixty-five years old when he was elected as Britain's prime minister in 1940. He was frequently seen with a huge cigar in his mouth, and many people referred to him as "Winnie." He had a very unusual way of speaking, and his voice was slow and deep. But he was always saying things that people quoted over and over to keep themselves cheerful and ready to fight. In his first speech as prime minister, Churchill said that the war would cost us our "blood, sweat, and tears," but that this was Britain's "finest hour." In a speech made after the soldiers had been safely evacuated from Dunkirk, he said that the British would continue to fight "by land and by sea and by air. . . . we shall defend our island, whatever the cost may be . . . we shall never surrender." Churchill's words gave people a lot of courage. Everyone thought that he was a wonderful leader.

It was Churchill who made the "V for Victory" sign popular. Whenever he appeared, he held up the first two fingers of his right hand in the shape of a V. He was never afraid of danger and always went out at night so that he could see the "fun," as he called the bombings. He had a special outfit designed for his nighttime outings. It was a jumpsuit in pale blue with a zipper up the front. It had a large pocket for the cigars that he loved to smoke. He called his outfit his "rompers," but the newspapers called it his "siren suit" because he always put it on the moment the sirens screamed. He wanted to save the precious minutes that it took to get into regular clothes.

King George was very brave, too. He never left London during the bombing and often went out to talk to the people in the areas that had been badly damaged. King George's home, Buckingham Palace, was bombed three times, but the bombs did very little damage to the building and no one was hurt. Many of the bombs dropped by German planes didn't explode. Every day, unexploded bombs were being dismantled and taken away all over London. It was extremely dangerous work. Some were buried so deep that they weren't found for many years, often when a foundation was being excavated for a new building.

Every Christmas Day King George made a speech to the people of Great Britain on the wireless. He had a terrible stutter when he spoke, but that made people like him even more. It made him seem like an ordinary man. When Princess Elizabeth was old enough, she joined the army and learned to repair lorries. Now she is the queen, and in her seventies, but she says that her favorite thing to do still is to repair lorries!

There were so many sounds and voices on the wireless that became symbols of the war. We heard them all again and again. Among them was "The White Cliffs of Dover," the most popular of all wartime songs. The white cliffs were what the airmen, soldiers, and sailors often saw last as they left England to go to battle. And what they saw first as they returned by plane or boat.

"The White Cliffs of Dover" was sung by Vera Lynn. She was so popular that she became known as "The Forces' Sweetheart." Her most famous song began,

"We'll meet again,
don't know where,
don't know when,
but I know we'll meet again,
some sunny day."

It always brought tears to everyone's eyes, including mine.

The German wartime favorite song, "Lili Marlene," was just as popular in England, where it had been re-recorded in English. The recording heard the most was sung by the American movie star, Marlene Dietrich. She was a German who had moved to the United States and was against what Hitler had done in Germany. Both songs made the people at home miss their husbands, boyfriends, sons, and brothers even more. I didn't like the song very much, or Marlene's accent, but I sang along like everybody else.

More than any other sound, the first notes of Beethoven's Fifth Symphony rang in everyone's head. The *Ba-Ba-Ba-Boom* began every wireless program. My parents explained that short, short, short, long is the Morse Code symbol for the letter V, and V stood for victory. Hearing those four notes always gave me goose bumps. Even on the sunniest day, it was hard to be optimistic about victory.

The Nazis added "Lord Haw Haw" to our wireless broadcasts on a regular basis. The actor was originally from England and had an affected English accent. He told the British people over and over how badly they were doing in the war. According to him, if they didn't want all of their men to be killed, they needed to surrender. People laughed at Lord Haw Haw, but they listened to him daily. After a while, they began to wonder if he were speaking the truth.

1944

The Yanks

In December 1941 the Japanese attacked the American naval base at Pearl Harbor, Hawaii. As a result, the United States declared war on Japan; then Germany and Italy declared war on America. The Americans (or "Yanks" as we called them) arrived in Lydney in the spring of 1944. With their crew-cut hairstyles, they weren't like the British soldiers. We all thought they looked most odd. And they always seemed to be chewing some strange stuff called "gum." We had no idea what it was, but we children all learned to say the sing-song phrase, "Got any gum, Chum?" if we met any soldiers in the town. We grew to like chewing gum very much.

The American soldiers' presence created a new concern: English men were worried that with the Yanks now based in so many towns, the supply of beer would soon be gone! The Americans hadn't brought any beer with them.

But they had brought lots of other things from America, and they were generous about giving them away. They gave the people of Lydney chocolate, cigarettes, razor blades (often none had been available), and many kinds of sweets ("candies," as we learned to call them). The ladies were given nylon stockings. No one had had stockings for years. Instead, women had painted lines on their legs so that people would think they were wearing stockings. In those days, stockings had a dark seam running up the back of each leg.

What we children craved the most were the chains from the G. I. "dog tags." These metal identification tags were stamped with each soldier's name, rank, and serial number and were worn at all times. But the soldiers seemed to have an endless supply of extra pieces of chain of various lengths, and a "dog tag" necklace or bracelet was a definite status symbol. It made you both different and special among your friends. Those who had sisters old enough to be the girlfriends of soldiers were the ones who usually got them. Because I didn't have a big sister, I never got a chain, which made me feel definitely underprivileged.

The W.V.S. did its best to make the Yanks feel welcome, encouraging families to invite them into their homes. The British were very appreciative of how much the United States was doing to help defeat the Germans, but food supplies were even shorter than before, and rationing made it difficult for the ladies to serve tasty meals. They were embarrassed by how little they had to offer, so U.S. army officials advised the soldiers to take food with them whenever they were being entertained.

About half a mile from our house was the Forest of Dean. It was a huge forest crisscrossed with dirt roads and winding trails, where sheep, by ancient law, were allowed to run free. All at once, each of the trails was marked with a signpost bearing American place names like CHICAGO and NEW YORK. Tents to house the soldiers, tanks, trucks, guns, and bombs were hidden among the trees. The forest, which until then had been a place of great beauty where we wandered freely and forgot for a while that there was a war on, became off limits for the local people. Like other Lydney families, we had often gone there for long, peaceful walks or to gather chestnuts in the autumn and wildflowers in the spring. Now our forest seemed dark and sinister with the secrets of war lurking among the dense trees.

1944

Flying Bombs

Even when there was no air raid warning, I often lay awake at night listening to the drone of the German Messerschmitt planes on their river route to the Midlands. They sounded so different from our tiny Spitfires and the larger Hurricane bombers. Each night I wondered about the people who would be killed or injured or would lose their homes. It was a terrible time.

British homes seldom had central heating. Like most of our neighbors, our main source of heat was the coal-burning fireplace in the living room. Every other room was icy cold at night in the winter except mine. I had a paraffin (kerosene) heater in my room. It was round, about two feet tall, and the pattern that was cut into the top cast a pretty design on my ceiling. As the oil burned, the pattern flickered, reminding me of a kaleidoscope. Some nights I stared at it for hours, sure that as long as I kept my eyes fixed on it, I would be safe. Until the V-1s, that is.

We had been hearing rumors for a year that the Germans were inventing a mysterious new weapon that would end the war. No one seemed to know exactly what it was, but I'm sure that everyone in England was as terrified as I was.

The V-1 was actually a flying bomb. Because of the sound they made, the newspapers and wireless were calling them "doodlebugs" or "buzz bombs." Their growling sound grew louder and louder as the bomb flew closer and closer to where you were. When it ran out of fuel, the engine spluttered, coughed, and then stopped. There was total, devastating silence as the bomb fell, followed by the roar of its explosion when it hit the ground. To me, it always sounded as if the engine had cut out directly overhead. The silence lasted for what seemed like a year, although it was really only a few seconds. I always lay rigid in my bed, holding my breath. At any moment I expected the bomb to make a direct hit on my house. The pattern on my ceiling became terrifying instead of beautiful. I was sure that the bomb would roar right through the center of that pattern, killing me instantly. But it never did.

From April 12, 1944, onwards, the Nazis sent a hundred V-1s over Britain every day. At first, when people saw their flaming tails in the night sky, they thought that the bombs were enemy planes on fire, so they cheered. But they didn't cheer for long. For two weeks the "doodlebugs" destroyed factories, homes, and families day and night. Because of radar, the British planes could sometimes detect and destroy a third of the bombs before they reached their targets, but that left an awful lot of them to do their damage.

The V-1 was followed by the V-2, which was even more destructive. Hitler expected the British people to surrender within a few days of the launch of the first V-1s, but they didn't. So he sent the V-2s. People were angry and frightened, but they were more concerned with building new houses than with surrendering to Hitler. Even though the war was more intense than ever, soldiers, sailors, and airmen were released from their duties for a while to help with the huge job of rebuilding. The government believed that the morale of the British people, especially of the homeless, was important.

1945

V.E. Day!

The war ended suddenly on May 7, 1945. At least it seemed sudden to me. I was ten years old. When we arrived at school that morning, we had no idea what an exciting day it would be. During the night our classroom had been damaged. There were bullets scattered everywhere. There was even a bullet hole right through Bob Windsor's desk. He became an instant hero! There had been no air raid sirens the night before, and we had heard no enemy planes. The attack was a mystery that was never to be solved.

And then at 11:00 A.M. we were told that the war was over. The Germans had surrendered! And no sooner did we hear the news, than the church bells began to peal. They had been silent for six long years. During the war church bells were to ring only to signal an invasion. We were given the rest of the day off and told that the next day, May 8, would be a national holiday. We couldn't believe our luck.

The wireless was calling it "V.E. Day—Victory in Europe Day."

I walked home from school that morning, alone. I found that I had a lot to think about. I passed a big poster that had been on the same brick wall for almost six years. I read it again, just as I'd read it every day since I'd learned to read:

YOUR COURAGE

YOUR CHEERFULNESS

YOUR RESOLUTION

WILL BRING

US VICTORY.

And it had!

Afterword

Sometimes as I was growing up, I felt I'd had no childhood. At other moments it seemed that my childhood had lasted an eternity. Either way, it had been a most peculiar period in my life. By the time the war was over, I couldn't remember a time when there hadn't been a war.

During the war, two hundred fifty thousand homes had been destroyed in London, and thirty thousand people had been killed. Those of us who lived in the country had been safer, and mine was one of the few families who didn't lose any family members or friends in the war. Sooner or later, after the war ended, they all came home. At first there were great celebrations; then life began to get back to normal. Rationing continued for a long time, and many foods were still scarce, but life without the scream of the sirens or droning of planes and V-2s overhead was like heaven.

I was to go to the grammar (high) school in September and would be there until I was eighteen. Like the rest of the

British people, the end of the war brought many changes for me. And all across the country, there was much work to be done. Houses, shops, and churches had to be rebuilt, and families had to readjust to having the men back home.

We learned afterwards that, without knowing it, we had been in considerable danger in Lydney. Only 9 miles away, beneath the small town of Chepstow, was a maze of tunnels. Throughout the war, surplus bombs had been stored in the tunnels. A stray German bomb landing there could have exploded them and killed us all.

Even closer to home, the Forest of Dean had become a munitions dump for the visiting Americans. The dirt trails that crisscrossed the forest all led to massive quantities of bombs, guns, and explosives. Some were hidden among the trees, while others were deep in old coal-mine shafts. If the Germans had dropped any bombs on the forest, it would have created terrible devastation. Fortunately, the one incendiary bomb that had landed there, leaving a huge crater, fell before the Americans arrived.

• • • • •

In 1970, twenty-five years after the war ended, we were again reminded of that time. A former German prisoner of war came back to England to visit our friends, the Windsors. They had been corresponding with each other through the years, and he returned to reclaim a watch the Windsors had bought from him when he was in England. They had kept it safe all those years, waiting for his return. Four other prisoners came with him.

In looking back on that period of my childhood, I have many memories of how the war changed the reserved British people. They helped and supported each other. They shared what little they had. They comforted those who received tragic news. They fought bravely and didn't give up. They treated their prisoners kindly. They laughed and cried together. And I was a part of it all.

Glossary

Even though people in Great Britain and the United States speak the same language, there are many common objects that are known by different words in each country. The following is a list of the British terms used in this book and their American equivalents:

BISCUIT   a cracker or cookie

CHEMIST'S   a drugstore; in Britain, a pharmacist is called a "chemist."

CINEMA   a movie theater

CLOAKROOM   a room or cubicle where outdoor clothing such as coats, boots, and backpacks are kept.

GARDEN   yard; a back garden is a backyard.

GUINEA   a British coin no longer in use. A guinea was worth one pound and one shilling.

KNICKERS   underpants for girls and women

LORRY   a truck

MATERIAL   fabric

PENCE   a British coin similar to our penny. There are twelve pence in a shilling.

PETROL   gasoline; it is a shortened form of the word "petroleum."

PETTICOAT   a slip

POUND (£)   the basic unit of the British money system, like the dollar in the U.S. system. A pound is worth $1.60 at this writing, but the rate of exchange varies.

PRAM   a baby carriage; it is a shortened form of the word "perambulator," which is a British name for a baby carriage.

RAILWAY LINES   train tracks

SWEETS   candy

SHILLING   a British coin similar to our dime. There are twenty shillings in a pound.

TEA   a hot drink served with milk; also, a meal served at 4:00 P.M. consisting of sandwiches, cakes, biscuits, jellies (Jell-o), tinned fruit, and tea. During the war, sugar sandwiches were a special treat for tea! In winter, when a warm meal was needed, "high tea" was often served at 5:00 P.M. instead. It was not a main meal and usually consisted of something on toast, such as a fried egg, baked beans, fried tomatoes, grilled cheese (this is known as "Welsh Rarebit"), or sardines. Kippers (smoked herring) with bread and butter were also popular. Dinner, the main meal, was traditionally served in the middle of the day. Now, many families have their cooked main meal in the evening, but customs vary from house to house and region to region. One British tradition that still continues: Promptly at 4:00 P.M., everything stops for a hot cup of tea and a biscuit or snack.

TIN   a can of fruit, vegetables, meat, coffee, tea, or other foods. The cans were originally made of tin.

WIRELESS   a radio

WOOL   knitting yarn

Further Reading

Borden, Louise. *The Little Ships: The Heroic Rescue at Dunkirk in World War II.* New York: Simon & Schuster, 1997, gr. 4 up.

Bunting, Eve. *Spying on Miss Muller.* New York: Clarion Books, 1995, gr. 1–8.

Cooper, Susan. *Dawn of Fear.* New York: Aladdin, 1989, gr. 5 up.

Drucker, Malka, and Michael Halperin. *Jacob's Rescue.* Hammond: Skylark, 1993, gr. 4–7.

Drucker, Olga L. *Kindertransport.* New York: Henry Holt & Co., 1992, gr. 5–8.

Foreman, Michael. *War Boy: A Country Childhood.* New York: Arcade, 1990, gr. 3 up.

Frank, Anne. *Anne Frank: The Diary of a Young Girl.* New York: Doubleday, 1967, gr. 7 up.

Greene, Bette. *Summer of My German Soldier.* New York: Dell, 1984, gr. 7–12.

Hahn, Mary D. *Stepping on the Cracks*. New York: Clarion Books, 1991, gr. 4–7.

Kerr, Judith. *When Hitler Stole Pink Rabbit*. London: Yearling Books, 1987, gr. 3 up.

Lowry, Lois. *Number the Stars*. Boston: Houghton Mifflin, 1989, gr. 5 up.

Margorian, Michelle. *Back Home*. New York: Harper Collins Juvenile Books, 1992, gr. 7 up.

Margorian, Michelle. *Good Night, Mr. Tom*. New York: Harpy Trophy, 1986, gr. 5–9.

Marx, Trish. *Echoes of World War II*. Minneapolis: Lerner, 1993, gr. 4–7.

Nolan, Han. *If I Should Die Before I Wake*. San Diego: Harcourt Brace, 1994, gr. 4–6.

Pearson, Kit. *The Sky Is Falling*. New York: Viking Kestrel, 1989, gr. 6–8.

Stevenson, James. *Don't You Know There's a War On?* New York: Greenwillow, 1992, gr. k–8.

Toll, Nelly. *Behind the Secret Window: A Memoir of a Hidden Childhood*. New York: Dial Books, 1993, gr. 5 up.

Vogel, Ilse-Margaret. *Bad Times, Good Friends*. San Diego: Harcourt Brace, 1992, gr. 5–7.

Westall, Robert. *Blitzcat*. New York: Scholastic, 1990, gr. 7 up.

Whitman, Sylvia. *V Is for Victory: The American Homefront During World War II*. Minneapolis: Lerner, 1992, gr. 5–12.

Index

(References to Britain, England, and the village of Lydney
run throughout the text)

Index

Index